WHITE LIGHTS
&
WHALE HEARTS

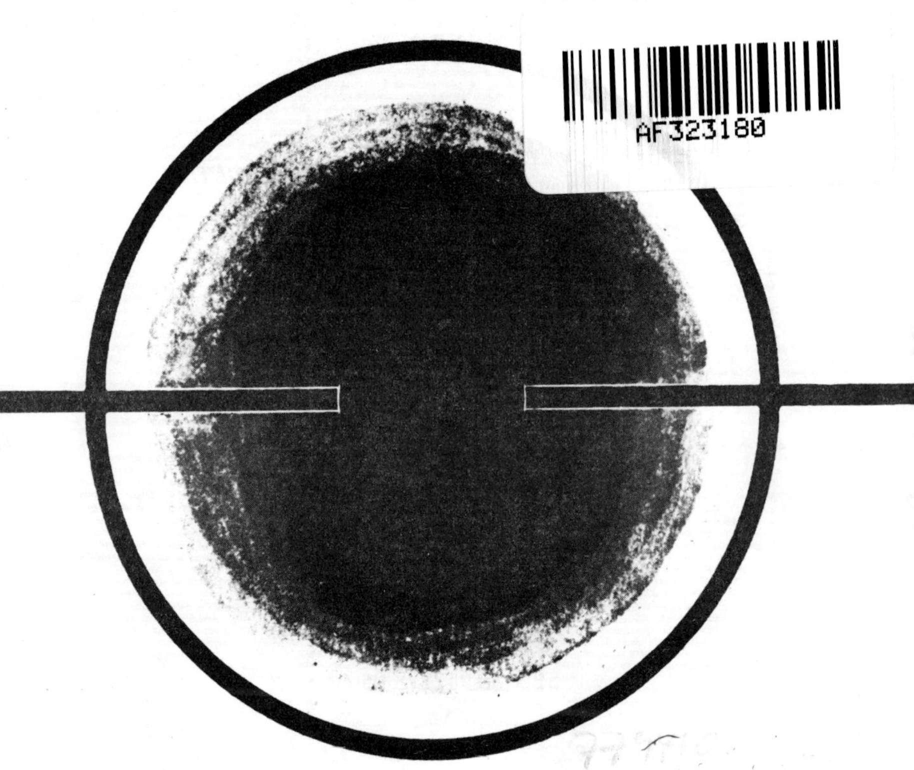

STEPHEN VINCENT

THE CROSSING PRESS, R.D. 3
Trumsnsburg, N.Y.

acknowledgements

HANGING LOOSE
NEW: AMERICAN AND CANADIAN POETRY

*Some of these poems
were originally published in the pamphlet,
PIECE BY PIECE (Redberry/Okike Pub-
lications, Nsukka, Nigeria, 1967)*

*The cover and illustrations
are by Donald Farnsworth*

SBN: 0-912278-05-6

CONTENTS:

ANTHEM

America, if you were a basketball court,
I'd double dribble down
all your edges. America, if you were a
basketball court, I'd take my shots
in every State. I'd begin with a foul
in Chicago, a set shot in Florida, a hook
in Alabama, and a jump shot in Washington.
O, America, I'd put hoops on all your edges,
backboards against every border and sea.
America, I would elbow across country kicking
my feet up and over every player in sight. America,
I'd give you naked cheer leaders, electric bands
and Referees guided by the strings
that hang down from the Justice of Heaven. America,
I'd name everybody as my players. The teams
would be bi-sexual and count women in the spring
of every step. We'd move so fast you wouldn't be able
to count the colors of our players. There would be such rhythm
that the Governor of every State would have to hide
in his box seat. The rafters would be loaded with lightening,
magnifying and giving life to each move, each pleasure.
We'd make this country move like a cyclone in Heaven,
the star white twirl of our ankles
would crack and clear
the trance of Death. Nevada and Virginia would be the locker rooms
out of which we would come storming with our underground passions
We'd have the tip-off in Kansas while the rooters swayed
to the rhythm of the Wizard of Oz, the fingers of the Centers touching
and turning the ball like the small eye
of the Gulf's tornado. On defense, we'd move from State to State,
keeping our hands moving like quick birds
or the breezes that tickle the slim stalks of wheat. On offense,
our bodies would move like ploughs insistent on breaking
the hard, spring ground. A chest pass over Nebraska,
fast breaks that we could steer through either Texas or Montana,
quick little lay-ups through Oregon and Idaho, or little Vermont
and Maine. A bounce pass through Oklahoma and Tennessee. Faking,
moving, stopping, elbowing, quick as possible, deft as
both the sparrow and the hawk, pressing our feet against the floor,
bringing our arms up, springing as high as we can, letting the ball leave

our finger tips in a high, slim arch, watching it slip through a dark rim
into the white strings
and out of the new net. It would be a great game. Children would be born
from the depths of our springs. A fall away jump shot would yield
to the embrace of mothers. The long overhead pass from one end
of the court to the other would provoke
a family reunion. O, America, the land of the living,
the land of the dead, the land of our yet unknown Gods
would be revealed through the terrible precision
of each of our moves. America, our heels charged with lightening,
our toes with sparks, we'd get all your States to nourish
each and every rooter. Loaves of bread and fish
would be on every corner. Your tired brown bleachers would be turned
into all the colors of the rainbow. America, America,
if you were a basketball court and this brought us so close
to Heaven, when the game was over, the sweat glimmering down
our silver spun bodies, America, we'd all slow down
and, as a finish to our efforts,
we'd bring Mick Jagger in,
and watch him dance, move and sing,
and, as the white lights
went out, putting our arms
around each other, we'd watch him
take a fine, straw broom
and begin to gracefully sweep
the whale hearts
off the whole length of the floor.

THE RESCUE

I didn't put the barb wire up,
she said from the other side
of the wall as I dropped the
blow torch, the chisel and the
hammer and reached for my
wire cutters and canvas gloves
and said, who in the hell
put up the bricks, the cement,
the metal plates and mortared
in these wicked chips of glass.
Don't ask me, she said, it
just started moving up on me,
you know, first one thing
and then another. Yes I know,
I said, and broke the wire
with a few stiff snips of the
cutter. And then I guess it got to
be an art with me, she said.
It's sort of fun, you know,
sticking these odd things
together. I used to go to the
dump daily to see what I
could find. Yes I know,
I said. Excuse me while I
chisel the brick and chip
the glass and try to pry
these metal plates away. I
might even have to use the
blow torch. I hope it's
worth it, she said. When I finish,
you better be undressed,
I said.

THE RELATIONSHIP

To be married,
to be a simple, smooth, loving thing:
that's what I wanted,
that's what I wanted.
But I could not give it to her,
no, I could not.
For me she would break apples,
make toasted cheese sandwiches
with thin slices of bacon,
and put paprika in the tea.
We would wake up at three;
I would get the oranges
she bought with thick skins,
and she would peal them
with a paring knife
and we would sit and make love
and eat them piece by piece.

Day and night she was with me.
Quiet or with or without talk.
In the day we would walk through the City park
and walk on our hands or crawl on our bellies
to tell the colors of the winter leaves.
In the evening as the sun went down,
we climbed stair-wells to look at chimney pots
and see them in their different child-like shapes
and I would recount what they had in common
with our, what I called, relationship.

And in the evening we would return
to our secret backyard flat and tell each other
favorite children stories that we thought
we knew the best until it came time
for us to get undressed. And this we did

week after week with hardly a pause
in this our merriment. Only once or twice
did she call me coward, pull the mustard
off the shelf and bloop it through the air/
curling the stuff around my head & throat.
                              But I got her back
you can bet, when she had to clean
the yellowed shirt.

Yet somehow it happened, I do not know why,
it came time to leave her from that
our backyard flat. Oranges, tea and sandwiches,
I could not give it back. She said it was my mother,
but I would not give in to that. And leave her,
yes I did, yes I did and yes I do, yes I do
regret the loss of her felicity,
                    the talk of marriage, children
and the lot. And in the evenings, you can bet,
I climb City stair-wells and sing this my song
to unmarried & single
chimney pots.

JEALOUSY

Go friendly, Go lovely, Go naked
My songs: the morning
Is for breathing. If you meet Eric
Tell him to get undressed. If you meet
Elizabeth, tell her I love her
And to get undressed. If you meet them
Together, help them get in bed:
Encourage their love and sleep.
And, if they ask of me, say
There is nothing between us.

ROLLINS

This man he pulls thru
the gorge. He's got a
strong neck and a full
belly. He's pouring it
straight. He's not afraid
to lay it on how it is.
He's my friend and your
friend but we are afraid
of him. Such is the law
of full statement. A man
who gives you what he has
gives you the rake
if you are not to be
what you have been.

JAGO IN SAN FRANCISCO

In Fillmore I yelled
to Othello
that he sustain in me
the abyss behind hate

and I spit of the licorice
winter there, awakened by the
quiet circle of the moon,
not taking it,

as I darted toward the pimp's
dark figure crossing
that street of cool macadam
for the hock shop -

and soon after
enjoyed my brown whiskey
and my throat tingled
with warmth

until morning
on the roofs of the ghetto
breathing blue
I questioned my hate, or

outside it wondered
if Othello loved me.

ON MY WAY TO TAKE OUT A BLACK GIRL

I begin to think I am black happy
        afraid to be torn
                with the words nigger happy
                    or gutter happy
                            or snipe happy.

The good ones
        tell me to keep away
                to push my cock
                        through softer bones,

tell me to get high
        on the Jewish girl
                or the Greek girl
                        but not the nigger girl

who they say is unhappy
        and stiff with the whore
                my father planted
                        in her mother's veins .

But I guess I am black happy
        unafraid of my father,
                a little wary
                        of her brother
                                my brother,

and without thinking
        of the purity
                of the woman
                        I call my mother.

And she,
        don't think she has plans
                for the navel scratch
                        or the belly itch
                                or whatever it is

dance or trip
        that the good ones tell me
                those people do
                        to forget gentlemen

like myself.   No
        I cannot know
                if she has fears
                        or plans or seeds of revenge
                                in the palm of her hand.

But if she is free,
        as I am free,
                I think it will be more
                        like the dance of lizards

you know, when the ground is so hot
        the secret way to survive
                is how to make your feet
                        touch and move
                                with an immediate art

across that terrible ground.

BACK TO BACK

He turned over
She turned over
Back to Back
He said She said
(touching their heels)
That was damn good

HYMN

TO A LOST FATHER

PROLOGUE

The ferry was defunct.
The wheel was broken.
The cables were rusty.
All day I sat out on the end
in a hard wooden chair
looking across the river.
In the afternoon I brought out
my viola d'amore, my rod &
my reel. And all afternoon
I looked across the river,
its smooth, untroubled expanse
while I played Vivaldi, fished
for leopard sharks & wondered
if my father/ would forgive me.

INVOCATION

Father/
You never look
at me. Taken
by your own
passion. You never
talk. I am left
a circle suspended
from the lake.
I am your design
left empty
circling you
like a hungry bird.
If you would
only
retrieve yourself
bring it up
bring it up
I would love you
half as much
stop singing
fill myself
and lie flat
on your belly
giving nothing
back.

THE BOAT

I remember when you built it.
I must have been three. It was out there
in the sideyard. The elaborate hull
held up and together by careful
scaffolding. The pure complications
of wood. It was poetry. Three miles away,
down at the Bay, they were building the ships
to go kill Japan. And there you were
on evenings and weekends working. I remember that.
I keep it in my head like the photograph of an
enlarged fingerprint. I keep it in my head
to push me while I am making this new poem.

TIME OF MY LIFE

Just once
you let me take the tiller
Just once
before you sold the boat
There I was
life-saver(orange)around
my twelve year old body
taking the Bear, POLA 8,
the red figure of the bear
and the number emblazoned
high on the sail. You told
me to watch the small blue
streamer to catch the edge
of the wind. I held on tight
with my right hand, the smooth
feel of pine & varnish. Across
from me, an early fifties can of beer
in your hand, you had a young smile
on your face talking to a friend
in the cock-pit. (Or was it my older brother
Mike, sea sick & half asleep?) The waves
were high, four o'clock in the afternoon,
the sun coming through the Gate, a nice wind;
I pulled the tiller a little too far to the
left, the silver spray leaped
over the hatch, the sails whined and the mast
shook as we keeled deep
to the wrong side, Angel Island already
coming into our head. For a moment I thought all
was lost, that we'd go over, capsised and drowning
into that green bay. But then, not thinking twice
I leaned back
on the tiller, lining the sail up
to the blue streamer and the wind. You
did not move once, but smiled and laughed
to the shake of beer in your can,
the sudden foam coming up to cover your lips
and laughed again, looking at me
as if you held me
and the whole wide world.

THE TURN

Those days I turned to hate you.
Going to school a sack of white yogurt
stuck in my throat. No longer
could I win the race running
across asphalt from curb to Eucalyptus.
I turned. I turned. My hands
gripped the wire on the Anchor fence.
My eyes traced the path of sea gulls
lifting up and down to take the orange peels
from the ground. In class, the sixth grade,
I turned to killing my first male teacher,
the man with the strange Yugoslavian name. Then
inscrutable, I turned to books and basketball
to acquire a whole new life. I was lost, lost
father. I turned to hate you, as if you,
yourself, had given up on
your very own name.

YOUR FATHER

I want to write about your father.
How he came from Oklahoma, first,
coming out on the train. Your mother's
brother tells me the story. He's still
from the Valley. A town called Arvin.
He's come to the house for Christmas dinner.
He begins the story. How he was working
for the railroad up above Fresno, a little place
called Hair Pin. And one day Johnny, your father,
gets off the train and comes quick hobblin'
up the road. He had a bad leg. How he too
gets a job with the railroad. I stop listening.
Hair Pin. My ear stops on Hair Pin. What a place
to begin, to start. Does it exist? No wonder
you all came down to Richmond,
the depot, the ferry and the water
to build your house
along the piers.

ANCESTORS

I can't write much more about
your father. I did not know him. All
I remember is that he had
high cheek bones
that your mother
tells me are Cherokee
and it is the
ghosts of these
entrances   high, solid and clear
the cheeks
that continue
to haunt me.

COMING UP & FALLING DOWN

You were brought up
on the edge of that bay. Boats, fish,
the sky, the moon,
you had your way
into all of them. You could stab bass
off the end of the ferry pier
(your daddy the time-keeper)
and flip them back
into your ol' lady's frying pan.
Everything was that close. Crystal sets,
model planes, houses, you were the
skinny Okie with hot nuts
to build everything. Already
a third boat by my birth.
How come it all had to come back down
in such a terrible way? Is it
because you lost and broke your plane
in a national contest
taking you back to Detroit
when you were only fourteen?
Or was it your father's hobble?
Come on. Let's go. I want an answer.

THE KNIFE

We were up on Eagle Creek. I was down
at the water cleaning a brown trout. You
had loaned me your knife to do the job.
I was in a hurry. The day before
the Rangers had killed six
rattlesnakes on the other side. I was
in a hurry. Later you asked
for your knife back. I could not find it.
Not in my pocket
or down by the creek. You were angry. Twenty
years, you said, with the same knife. And now
I had gone and lost it for good. What kind of
boy was I? At first I was sad, sad for you
and your lost knife like you had lost
a close friend. But then I was happy. I don't
know why. I went back up
to the camp fire and cooked and ate
my beautiful fish. I even ignored the buzz
and the terror of the yellow jackets. I was that
happy.

BASKETBALL

I never let you come to the games. I never
invited you. You never asked. You never
saw me on the court handle the round skin
of the basketball. You never came to see me
spread my warm fingers like the edges of stars
around the ball as I went like a smooth fox
down the court my tennis shoes squeaking faster
than a grasshopper through clover. At sixteen
I travelled fast
father. Lay in, set shot, jump shot, bounce pass,
chest pass, bucking, elbowing as high as I could,
reacher for what was never given, the smooth flow
of the ball arching high towards the rim, its high arc
lifting subtly down, a smooth swish through
the star shapes of the unbroken
white net. Let me play that game again. I was on the court
with Willie, Leroy, Hobo & Sam. I the only white
with four blacks. Don't get me wrong. I was scared of them
as you of me or I of you. But it began. Somebody
poked me in the eye, it stung, and I released everything
travelling up and down the court a young man
with a quick gun and a sharp elbow. For the first time
we held together like a rapid running loom weaving
up and down between the other players who held together
stiff as strings as we broke through all their empty
edges. Suddenly it was no game. Perfect harmony
of movement and song. The referee could blow no whistle.
In victory I always refused you
entry. This time
I am going to win.

SMALL CHANGE

One day you called me a 'chicken shit'.
I could not get from 'low' into 'second'
going up a high hill. We were in my
brother's truck. You were helping me
move to the City. When the clutch slipped
and the truck fell back
into the car behind you called me
a 'chicken shit'. That day
I had the most energy
of my whole life. Beginning that
day I didn't come home
for a whole month.

THE DAY I LEFT HOME

The day came & the bus
was out front. Long and shiny.
The driver was dispassionate,
only a concern for time. I got on
at 12:42, closing the door
behind me. We were due to leave
at 12:45. At 12:44 I realised
I forgot my lunch and radio.
I told the driver to wait a minute.
These were valuable if I was to really
make my journey. I charged back
into the house and retrieved
the special baggage. However, this time out
the door would not close. SLAM SLAM
I slammed it again and again. It had warped
into a slender bough
and would not
fit the lock. Desperately I looked
towards the driver. He gave me
a, 'Sorry buddy. I already have to
reverse my schedule' and turned the bus
around and left in the opposite
direction. Finally I gave the door
one big heave
and pull until it came clean
and shut. It was clear
I would not be taking any
bus. My baggage gripped firmly
in my hands, the radio antenna flashing
into the air I began to walk
suddenly aware
of my own tenuous weight
the remote sun and the declining house,
retreating to the North,
its shadow still
casually flowing
into my back.

MOTHER

Everytime I leave you
and approach her
she that will give me entry
give me design
Everytime I leave you
hoping to face and touch
warm earth
Everytime when the spell
is so deeply upon me
I hear your voice
    calling me back
    calling me back
not quietly, not softly
not in gentle or happy mourning
but a strident
    'bring him back alive
    'bring him back alive
as if you were the Greek mother
from the balustrade of the fortress
pleading to the Senior Officers
that I not go into battle
or, as if, in your eyes
without you, death would be
my one and only
possible
chore. No,
mother. I have left,
though begging, I float
like a swan
over 30
white lakes.

CHANT

Father, Father, Father
Father unto myself
Father unto the moon
Father unto the sun
Father Father Father
I yield unto my breast
unto myself unto the sky
unto unto unto unto
Father I am the Father
Ghost Ghost Ghost
I keep looking out the window
The Resurrection
Father Father Father
Unto myself Father Father Father
To make myself holy To make myself pure
Father Father Father
Unto myself the kick into the air
the kick forward Yield
when only absolutely necessary
Father Father Father
The crime bleeds The spirit continues
Father Father Father
Yearn Yearn Yearn
I hold my hands forward
with a large sweep
Father Father Father
Give unto me Give unto me
Myself Myself Father Father Father
Unto myself Unto myself the Father the Father
I am
The Father

HOW IT IS

My left knee
is talking to my right knee
and my face is crying.
My feet begin
to move gently
as if death
were flowing
underneath. My left knee
is talking
to my right knee. They are both
hard and durable. They are saying
there will be war
for the next
five years.

REQUIEM

I watch the roses float
upon the sea
a wreath
for my mother her bosom
unleashing all that was given
all that was forbidden
her four sons, my father
and me.

ENVOI

This story sprouts in my conscience
like blood. The rose red flower
of my being. Do not bend me.
Do not break me. Remember the flood.
Remember the flood. I am blessed
with the right to kill
when forsaken. No. I am blessed
with the right. Treat me
as a flower. Do not bend
or bite. Choose what you feel
is more than ordinary, reject
what is contrary, pick what you do
pick it just right

THE ENEMY

It's time to write a poem
about the enemy. That little son-of-a-bitch
who ain't worth a mother's tinker's damn
who everyday gets in the way with his mouth
with his hands with his feet with his belly
you know who I mean when a hot flash gets going
and words begin to go and there he comes around
the corner like a Kamikazee fighter his wide
ugly mouth open his venomous teeth out and just
as you're ready to not only register that large white
boat come flowing by, but you really want to get
on it this time and take that white flash fully
guided high fever boat over the wave flow:
there the little son-of-a-bitch goes with his mouth
like a snake fang into your left palm and you're
left screaming there hot and heavy wondering
what in the hell hit, why and how we gonna get rid
of this heavy mother fucker. As that boat goes
right on by.

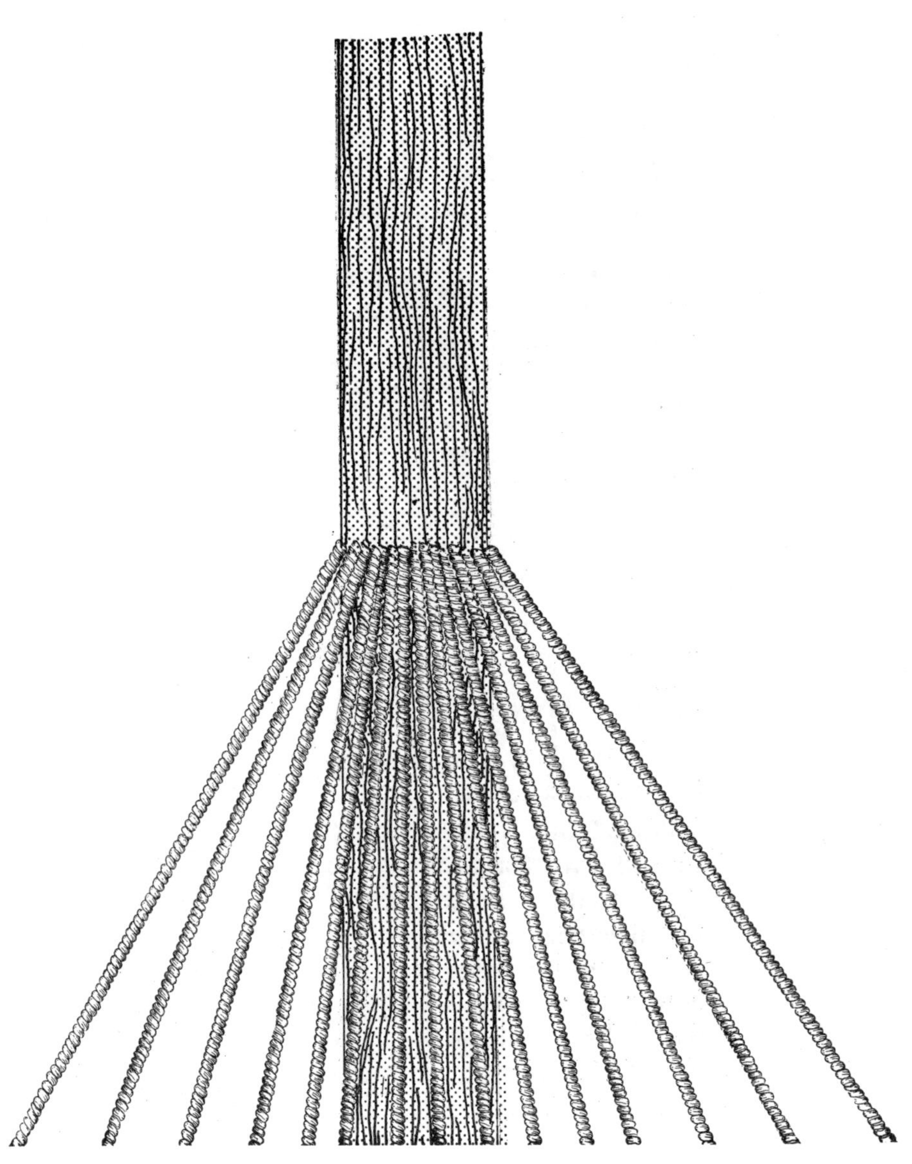

HOLD ON NOW

Turn I turn to love you
Father
You are
my father
christened in the woods
green birth of my beginnings
debts and debtors
we should not burn ourselves
on a small cross:
black bats might spin
from my hip bone,
bitter squalor
from the bitten tongue
I thank you for craft
I thank you for the eye
that intersects the left
to right the mighty opera
hidden in your heart
the wayward lust that must bend you
into your winter season
I beg you hold on
give birth to no other
but the songs of me
and my brothers. Hold on
we will carry you on
to the birth
of a new boat, a new sea,
pure forms for father and son,
pure song, mast up,
the seed I am sailing
into the colors
of a new weave.

ANNIVERSARY OF THE HYMN

In the dream it is an illumination. Sunshine and afternoon
down at the Bay. I pull into the dockyard of the Boatworks
and harbor where my father kept his boat. I'm driving my red
Japanese station wagon. I get out in front of the rail ramp where
the boats are pulled up for dry dock and refinishing. I hear a
scraping sound. When I look behind me, my father's Bear boat
has slid off the top of my car on to the ground. (Naturally, un-
der real circumstances, the boat would not have fit on top of the
small foreign car, or any car, for that matter). Nevertheless I look
out to the docks to the particular berth where we once kept the
boat. It is empty. Suddenly I hear my father's voice say, you have
stolen the boat from the man to whom I sold it. You should re-
turn it to him. At the moment I'm thinking it's going to be dif-
ficult to move the boat off the dry gravel back down into the
water and over into its proper berth.

I look up into the Eastern sky. In what was just pure blue an
immense cast iron pot is spinning through the air. It is foaming
and smoking up with what I automatically assume to be sulphuric
acid. It spins to the North, its fluids dripping over the side, until
it hovers over the black steeple top of my parent's house, where
it tips half way over and lets the boiling liquid spill on to the
house, turning it into immediate flame, thin flickering high flames
that are devouring the place.

Suddenly the whole family is with me:mother, father, Michael,
David, Chris. We think it's too late to recover anything, there,
where we are standing on the edge of the Bay. But, just as sud-
denly, like the flame in Moses' bush, the fire is extinguished. All
of us are back in the house, in the high attic. The roof is still on.
Burning has taken some of the stuff, but we are quickly, almost
joyously, going through the ashes, picking through all our family
relics, saving what can be saved. I'm grabbing up my diaries from
childhood.

Michael, my older brother, finds a picture of me and laughs. I
look at it. I look eighteen, but I have a pirate style moustache
waxed up into curves like an antelope's horns. I never had such a
moustache and, at eighteen, couldn't have grown one. Mike's laugh
is one of ridicule, the way he used to poke fun at me. But I'm not
put down by it and hurt, as in the past. There, in the attic, I feel
I have achieved manhood. I toss the photo away and laugh, too, at
the adolescent mask I must have once tried to assume.

This is the end of the dream of the end of my life in the house.

THE SONG OF THIS HOUSE

It's November
and I have the first hole
ever in the sole
of my left, big brown boot.
It's November
and I have to junk the car
the transmission is shot
beyond repair. It's November
and I'm chanting
I want love I want love
We've swept the dust
out of the house
cleaned all the laundry
ordered dry goods,
vegetables and chickens.
And I'm screaming
I want love I want love
I open my heart
like the slippery pages
of the telephone book
numbers I am full of numbers
and addresses and Cities
all over the bay
and I am breathing
I want love I want love
Bottle of glue, key chain
all these passionless objects
that surround a body
full of blood beating, flesh
attentive and hungry
and I'm moaning
and groaning I want love
I want love   The moon
is in retreat the sun
left hanging my typewriter
falls thru the desk
down down I follow it
I follow it into the night
into the dark I am lost
Where are you
It's November
and I'm waiting.

ELEVATOR LANDSCAPES

FIRST

I got on here.
I look out.
I see 20 hats.
I see 10 faces.
I see 5 necks.
I see 2 sets of shoulders.
I see no
immediate way
out of here.

BASEMENT

First there is darkness.
Second
the ignition of concrete:
the fear of death.
Illuminated green fish appear.
We suck with all
the strength of our bellies.
They enter us, one by one,
like soft sex.
We begin to rise.
A second door closes.

FOURTH

Everybody gets out
except me. I stretch
my arms, rub my belly,
bend over and
touch my toes. It is nice
to know myself
on such
intimate
terms. A girl, my age,
walks on. Her left foot
touches my
right one.

FIFTH

She does not talk.
I pull my left
shoulder back.
I carry an orange
in my left
arm pit. She has
a bird in the cage
of her back. The two
are in the middle
of a conversation.
Orange to bird. Bird
to orange. I am
deeply jealous. My lips
are sealed
like sour artichokes.

EIGHTH

She is holding steady.
You have to say hello
to acknowledge what
is already habit
between bird
and orange. The door
opens. There is a
large rock. Page 22
out of a Hulk
comic. The image
of cosmic disaster. Or
great things
to come. Your fingers
already
caressing the small craters.
Both of you
acknowledge this
by revealing
your tongues.
Night flames appear
as if across a whole
oil refinery.

TENTH

I take this moment
as intermission
for my father. His humor,
still tenuous and unsure,
his need
for compassion. My brother
who
because of the cycle
of beginnings and endings
will some day
punch him
in the mouth. There is actually
no such
cycle. We forever
punch each other
in the mouth. The
door opens. My father
does not appear.
Darkness. I am discovering
a deep need
to discover
the seed
in myself. My cock twitches
like a limbering
willow.

ELEVENTH

She leans against the numbers
on the panel like
a woman who looked like
Rita Hayworth leaned on
a parking meter in Richmond
in 1942. Dorthea Lange
caught that. The woman,
probably from the South,
waiting for her ol' man
to get off work at the
Kaiser Shipyard. Or
maybe just waiting.
I'm catching this
as the door opens
into eleven guitar players
levelling out
a monstrously quiet
music.

TWELFTH

Whenever she gets off
I'll get off.
Whenever she gets on
I'll get on.
This is a closed form
of argument. The orange
is peeling, the bird
is pecking and this is
a senseless form
of checking. The door slides
into an open field
of green clover. I'm rolling out
like a spinaker
turned over, a large cup
to receive her. We grow up
like Venus
taking off
her contact lenses.

FOURTEENTH

Quiet moment
like summer vacation.
A soft brown deer
with white specks.
A young buck without
responsibility. He actually
draws our contempt.
We are talking to each other
now. Serious signs
of possible agreement.
I let you punch
all the buttons
except the basement.
I am rising
in the memory
of green fish.

FIFTEENTH

The first argument.
A failure of pronouns.
I, You, Me, We.
We open on a landscape
of sandblasted
French cathedrals. The
stained glass windows
are breaking and falling out
in tears that become
grenades. We lay each other
flat with each
droplet. I'm exploding
with desire to deepen
the breach. It is across
the darker abyss'
that I love
to reach. (The sound
of black inside
the circle
of rose).

On this floor
there are no numbers.
We walk out
beyond their civilisation.
Five kangaroos, four of them
are coupling
each other. The fifth
nods that we enter
them like fresh meat
into lovely sandwiches.
I'm drawn to your couple,
you're drawn to mine.
We are not at war
with each other.
I'm just rolling & rocking
between two kangaroos
that love every inch
of my body. They take me
to a rubbing heighth
until there is a low
moaning sound
out of my belly
like the whistling wail
across a telegraph wire
crazing a message
thru the middle
of winter. I cannot hear you
but hear you scream
with malevolent delight.
My mind zeroes

into a searing blank.
I come out of it
pouring the sound
of white juice.
My kangaroo lovers
liberating me
from their hot brown
fur. We meet each other
cleansed from a new light
as the fifth kangaroo
rubs an empty pouch
and nods us
back in thru
those open doors.

SEVENTEENTH

Is this the elevator?
The thing that takes us
up and down. Seventeen.
Superior completion. A
child is born. The end of
certain obscenity. The snake
swallows the tail,
the whale takes in
the unskilled
fish. My hand goes smack
against the wall.
All the numbers flash.
A door opens
on a white volcano.
We are taken
by the breath
of subtle ashes. I
don't like the way
we are going. I pull you
into my arms
and the door closes.
We move into
a diminishing
but fertile
chapter. A baby
is born. All my wishes
are shorn. It is the end
of shallow sheep. Together
we begin
to weep.